winning
tennis doubles

winning
tennis doubles

Cynthia and Peter Doerner
with Dan Ozier

cbi Contemporary Books, Inc.
Chicago

Library of Congress Cataloging in Publication Data

Doerner, Peter.
  Winning tennis doubles.

  Includes index.
  1. Tennis—Doubles.   I. Doerner, Cynthia, joint
author.   II. Ozier, Dan, joint author.   III. Title.
GV1002.8.D63   796.34'228   77-91151
ISBN 0-8092-7697-6
ISBN 0-8092-7696-8 pbk.

Cover photograph: Jacquelyn Kilpatrick
Mixed doubles photographs: Sam Castro
Men's doubles photographs: Jacquelyn Kilpatrick

Copyright © 1978 by Peter and Cynthia Doerner
All rights reserved
Published by Contemporary Books, Inc.
180 North Michigan Avenue, Chicago, Illinois 60601
Manufactured in the United States of America
Library of Congress Catalog Card Number: 77-91151
International Standard Book Number: 0-8092-7697-6 (cloth)
                                    0-8092-7696-8 (paper)

Published simultaneously in Canada by
Beaverbooks
953 Dillingham Road
Pickering, Ontario L1W 1Z7
Canada

contents

Contents

acknowledgments

Our thanks to Jim Demas, Bob Cherry, Danny Krebs, John Williamson, Lynn Blumberg, and Dan Ozier for participating in our photographs.

Peter and Cynthia

introduction

Doubles, long considered the stepchild of the game of tennis, is a team sport that generates a great deal of spontaneous spectator response. The energy and excitement generated by doubles play creates an electric atmosphere that turns on spectators and involves them directly in the game.

As court space becomes increasingly hard to come by and more players and spectators learn to appreciate the intricacies of doubles, the beauty of its movement, the special skills required, and the synchronized thought and action demanded by such a team sport, the greater the role doubles will play in the overall tennis scene.

This book is designed expressly for the player who already understands the diverse complexities of the game of tennis and wishes to increase his knowledge of the game of doubles. At the same time, it serves as an instructional guide for coaches, physical education instructors, and teachers at all levels of education where players are taught and developed.

It is our intent to present the finest text possible to assist you in becoming a better informed, more complete master of the game of doubles. *Winning Tennis Doubles* teaches you not only where and when to hit a shot, but also why you should hit it there. The emphasis is on *tactics.* Every top professional knows why he hits the ball where he hits it and knows what to expect after he has made the shot. Without this knowledge and understanding he would be unable to plan his strategy or be prepared for the unexpected. We have incorporated the thoughts and ideas of professional tennis players into *Winning Tennis Doubles* in order to bring you to that same level of comprehension. *Where, when,* and *why* constitute the "guts" of this book. This total approach to the game makes *Winning Tennis Doubles* the most comprehensive instructional book in its field on the market.

Throughout this book you will be challenged to use the "triangle." We call it magic, but in fact it is a concept well grounded in the fundamentals of the game and is possibly the most important concept presented in this book. The triangle is basic to any ball game played on a rectangular surface. As most tennis players know, a thorough knowledge of angles is essential to developing a winning game. It is for this reason that we have chosen to emphasize the triangle.

In doubles the idea is always to assume a position on the court that establishes partners as two points at the base of a triangle with the ball serving as the third point. Whether on offense or defense, positioning yourself in the triangle will put you in the best possible court position.

Study the diagrams and text with care. When you have a complete understanding of both, you will have all the mental tools you need to become an accomplished doubles player. Then you will realize what we mean when we say the triangle is magic.

winning
tennis doubles

chapter one

the server

The game of doubles is played on the singles tennis court extended on each side by an alley four and one-half feet wide. Doubles is emphatically a team sport. It demands that partners match their wits, wisdom, skill, tactics, and psychology against their opponents. The object of doubles, as in any other sport, is to win. Winning requires a complete understanding of all aspects of the game, dedication to the perfection of the skills involved, and an appetite for keen, aggressive play. Doubles is a game of attack. You must attack the ball, the net, and your opponents' game. The only thing you do not attack is your partner. Your partner is your teammate, your confidant, and your fellow winner or loser, and he therefore deserves your kindness,

1

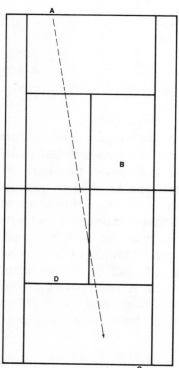

All four players are in proper position for the serve. Player A serves tightly to C's backhand.

understanding, encouragement, and all of your positive thinking while on the court. These considerations are of more importance that the skill it takes to play the game. You cannot play the game at all without your partner, so help him and let him help you.

POSITION

For the serve, assume a position on the baseline exactly one-half the distance between the center of the court and the outside alley line. This position has many advantages: it centers you in your half of the court, gives you the best opportunity for service placement, lets you serve over a lower point of the net from the even court, and allows you to move the shortest possible distance to the point where you can best volley the return of serve.

Tactics

The first volley should start from one foot behind to (preferably) one foot in front of the service line. Volley down the middle, just out of reach of the netman. After you make the volley, follow behind the flight of your ball to a point nearer your partner, who will have adjusted his position in relation to your volley. His position is now almost directly in front of the ball and you are even with him at his right, establishing the triangle. The triangle places you and your partner in the best possible position for the best possible return.

The placement of the serve is infinitely more important than the speed of the ball. This does not mean, however, that you should dink your serve to insure placement, because that will only set your partner up for a ball in the teeth. You can avoid this unpleasantness by hitting your first serve to your opponent's backhand with good pace and spin. As a matter of fact, it is a good idea to think backhand eighty to ninety percent of the time. If you have developed a big, flat serve that you're dying to

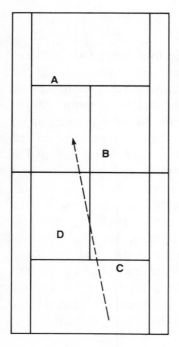

Player A has served to the backhand of C, who returns crosscourt out of reach of the offensive netman and follows his return to the net. A, moving in quickly behind his service, prepares to volley the shoulder-high forehand. B and D altered their basic positions when C returned service.

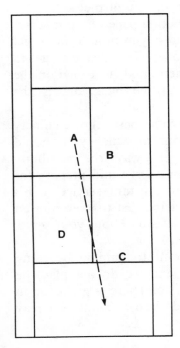

Player A closes in on the return and volleys down the middle for a winner. B moves toward the net. C and D are trapped.

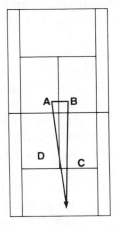

A and B form the base of the triangle. The ball is the third point.

use, save it for singles. In doubles you should take about one-quarter of the speed off your hard, flat serve and add a little spin for safety, comfort, and effectiveness.

A three-quarter-speed, spinning kicker to your opponent's backhand will cause him lots of problems. First of all, the backhand is usually the weakest of the basic strokes among club players, so it behooves you to attack that weakness. A player must be very quick to hit the return of service off his backhand. He has to make all the physical adjustments preparatory to hitting it and still have time to hit out in front if he is to hit it well. When you also mix it up with dashes of "spin in," "spin out," and "kicking high," the receiver will soon be looking for a racquetball court in which to ease his frustrations. By strategic serving you can own your opponent physically and, perhaps more importantly, psychologically. He knows that he not only has to hit the serve and hit it well, but he must also get it safely past your netman while at the same time keeping it low so that you will not have the opportunity to cream his partner.

There are also strategic reasons for taking pace off your serve. A three-quarter-speed, kicking serve allows you more time to get to the net and make a more effective volley. The idea is to get to the net as quickly as possible, camp there, and hit *down* on the ball. The three-quarter-speed kicker to the backhand is the answer.

Although this serve is generally your best choice ninety percent of the time, there are situations in which you should break the pattern. For example, there is always the possibility that your opponent will get wise to your serve and prepare for it. When he begins to groove on your constant service to his backhand, slip him one wide to his forehand just to keep him on his toes. As long as he has to make a decision about your serve, you have the advantage.

There are times when you might want to gamble by using your big serve. We are not machines, and we do not play the game mechanically, nor would we want to. There is great fun in gambling and winning, so take the odds into account and play the percentages and gamble.

The odds for using your big serve are in your favor at the beginning of a match, when you are fresh and your opponents do not know what to expect. If you should happen to serve an ace, you may not need to try it again during the match. You can bet that your opponent will be thinking about the ace for the rest of the match, and his thinking about it is to your advantage. If you go for the big one and serve a fault, then place the second serve to your opponent's backhand.

You can usually gamble when the score is 40-love in your favor and occasionally when the score is 40-15. If the gamble pays off, you will have ended the game with an ace, thereby destroying your opponent psychologically. And if the big serve fails you, you still have a one- or two-point advantage to work with to recover your losses.

There is one final situation in which you might occasionally choose to change the pattern of your service. Break the rule occasionally on pressure points if your opponent has a clear stroke preference or an obvious weakness or is known to choke on pressure points. Your knowledge about your opponent is one of the most effective weapons you have. Use it. You will know when you have him down. You can tell by the score, by his court conduct, by the comments he makes to himself or others, or by how and when he changes his game. The feeling is intangible, but it is just as real as if you could hold it in your hand. Couple that feeling with the knowledge of where you are in the game and set; then let him have it.

As the server, you are in the best position to see every player position on the court. Make use of this vantage point by noting the positions taken by your opponents and deciding in advance where to hit the volley off the return of serve. No matter what position your opponents take, you, as server, must get to the net and establish the triangle.

To use the concept of the triangle, think of yourself as being connected to your partner by an invisible bar that keeps you a fixed distance apart. You can determine the length of this "invisible bar" as follows: You and your partner should stand facing the same way. Position yourselves so that the racket

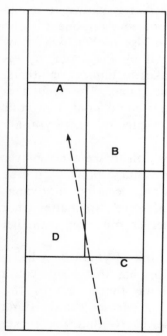

Player A moves into perfect
position in preparation for the
return of service. B and D move
with the volley.

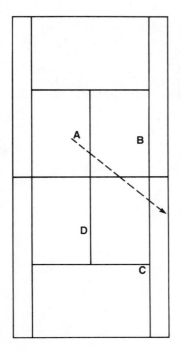

Player A, attacking, gets to the ball before it can drop and volleys crosscourt in front of C for the winner. B moves over to guard the alley. Note that A and B finish the point in the triangle, side by side.

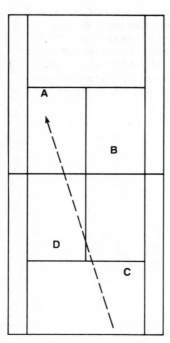

C has placed a medium-paced return crosscourt, and A stoops to pick up the volley with his forehand. C is coming in behind his return, and B will begin his move toward the center of the court.

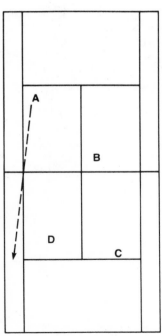

Player A picks up the volley and
sends it down the alley for the
winner. D is too late. C is out of
play. A and B will follow behind
the volley, ending the point side
by side with A near the alley
and B just across the center
line.

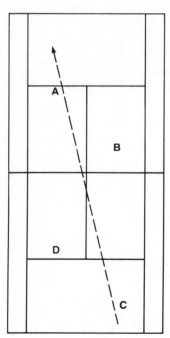

C lobs over A's head as A comes in behind his serve. B starts back to join his partner as C and D move toward the net.

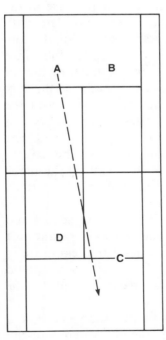

Player A goes up for the overhead as B sets up the base of the triangle by his side. They will come to the net behind the smash. D is in the best defensive position, but C is trapped on the service line as the ball goes between them for a winner.

heads are almost touching when you extend your rackets straight out to the side. This is the distance that ensures the best position both offensively and defensively. When your partner moves, you move at the same time, always maintaining the same distance between you. This will be true for all four players on the court, so it is best to keep in mind that when one player hits the ball, four players move.

Every time you prepare to serve the ball, you have the choice between hitting it hard and placing it well. You should most of the time choose placement over speed. Remember that the harder you serve the ball the faster it comes back at you. A hard, flat serve will most of the time come back fast so that it may keep you from joining your partner at the net, attaining the best position for volleying, and establishing the triangle.

If your serve is weak and you decide to stay back on the baseline, you will have to take a crosscourt return off the ground before you can join your partner at the net. If the receiver has come to the net behind his return, he and his partner are in the best offensive position (the triangle), and you are left with having to pull off an exceptional passing shot or go for the lob. If you are faced with this decision, we recommend the lob, since it gives you the chance to join your partner at the net or him to join you at the baseline, depending on the altitude of the lob. Either way, you will have found each other and will be in the best possible position given the circumstances. If you get out of the point alive and manage to get out of the match in one piece, consider it a learning experience, one that should send you to the practice court to work on your serve. Remember, the name of the game is attack, attack, attack, and you cannot attack without a serve that is an offensive weapon.

On the other hand, if the receiver hits the ball crosscourt and chooses to stay back, both teams are in the awkward position of having one man up and one man back. At least the teams are in equally bad positions. Obviously, the first short ball should bring the back man to the net, to his partner, and to the triangle. That is the place to be.

The object of serving for placement rather than speed and following in behind the serve is to get to the net, where you can hit down on the ball. Any return that might come back after

14

that will find you and your partner in the triangle, the best possible position for interception and attack.

So choose your three-quarter-speed kicker, follow quickly to the net, volley crisply down the middle, and get your team off to the best possible start.

THE WHOLE THING ONE MORE TIME:

1. Serve from one-half the distance between the center of the court and the outside alley line.
2. Follow service in a straight line toward the net.
3. Volley from inside the service line, if possible.
4. Follow the line of the ball until you are even with your partner, establishing the triangle.
5. Choose placement rather than speed when serving.
6. The backhand is usually weaker. Attack it.
7. Spin the serve to your opponent's backhand.
8. Keep your partner alive and well.
9. Place eighty to ninety percent of your serves to the backhand.
10. A three-quarter-speed serve causes physical and psychological problems for the receiver.
11. Mix up your serves when the receiver grooves on your kicker.
12. Continue a winning service placement.
13. Go wide to the forehand if the receiver moves to the backhand side.
14. Gamble early, while you are fresh.
15. You can usually gamble at 40-love and occasionally at 40-15.
16. Stay in the triangle until the point is over.
17. When one player hits the ball, four players move.
18. Stay at the net until driven back by a lob.
19. Lob when you are in trouble.
20. Come to the net on the first short shot if you have stayed back after the serve.
21. Be at the net to hit down on the ball.
22. Encourage your partner.
23. Practice your serve and volley.

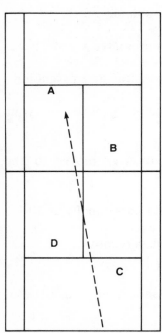

C returns the serve down the middle. A corrects his direction and moves toward the ball. B moves toward center court as D anticipates the volley and moves in to intercept.

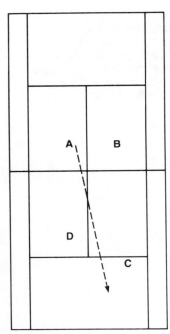

Player A closes quickly and volleys the backhand down the middle in front of D, finishing the point side by side with B in the best court position, the triangle.

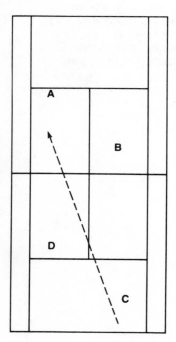

C hits a medium-paced crosscourt return and follows in along the path of the ball. A prepares for the volley. B steps toward center court as D moves in. Note how A gets in low to volley.

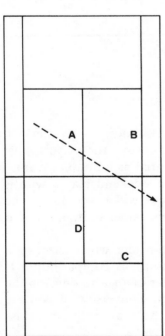

A hits a soft drop shot crosscourt into the alley. B moves over to cover any possible return. C and D change direction, with C heading for the ball and D covering center court. A is following behind his shot and will be in the triangle when the point ends.

chapter two

the offensive netman

Frequently, even at the professional level, a doubles partner will be selected at the last minute. When this occurs, the players have slight chance of playing up to their potential as a doubles team.

The "pick-up team" is all right for the weekend player who is just out for some fun and exercise, but it will never do for the serious player interested in developing his game. Partners should always be picked for a long term.

There are many factors one should consider when selecting a partner. First, and perhaps most important, is compatibility. If you get along well, you will have a better chance to develop the skills you have and put them into effect. Conversely, if you are incompatible, no matter how skillful you are you can kiss teamwork, harmony, and winning good-bye.

CHOOSING A DOUBLES PARTNER

It is extremely important to find a partner whose mind and game complement your own. With this comes a mutual respect for the other player and his ability, which in turn leads to harmony, teamwork, and winning. Two good players who know, understand, and respect each other and who work together as one will usually beat the socks off two singles superstars who persist in playing their own individual games in doubles competition. It should be emphasized that doubles is a team sport and must be played *with* a partner, not in spite of him.

DECIDING WHO TAKES
THE BACKHAND COURT

Once you have chosen a partner, you will have to decide who is the stronger player in order to determine which side each of you will play. Many people believe that the player with the better backhand should play the odd, or ad, court. Let us get rid of that idea right now. The stronger player, meaning the one with the better all-around game, should play the backhand.

Many pressure points, including 15-30, 30-40, and most game points, are played on the backhand side. At 4-all in a nine-point tiebreaker, the receivers have choice of sides, and they should elect to receive from the backhand side. Now the receiver has an advantage since the server knows he is serving to the stronger player and knows he must serve wide, over a higher point of the net. The pressure is tremendous, and the receiver has as much in his favor as possible.

POSITION

Take your position six to eight feet from the net, halfway between the center service line and the inside alley line. This places you in the best position to guard your half of the court, close enough to the net to hit down on the ball, and within one step of being in position to cover the point of most returns, the center of the court at the lowest point of the net. Be ready.

21

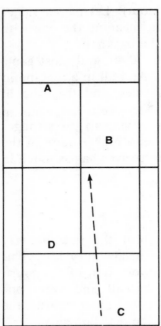

C returns the serve down the middle but gets it up too high. B steps toward center court to cut it off. D knows he is in trouble and holds his position, preparing for the worst. Player A sees his partner poach and continues toward the net.

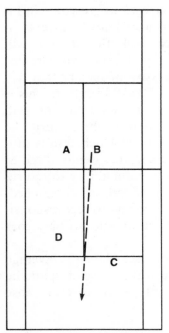

B follows through after hitting down on the ball directly between his opponents. A joins B at the net. C is trapped in no-man's-land, and D never had a chance.

TACTICS

When you take your position, you will find the receiver almost directly in front of you. This means that he must have you in his eye while concentrating on your partner, the server, while he serves. Your mere presence there makes you an obstacle. You are someone to be avoided, yet he must keep you in his mind, because if he forgets for one instant that you are there, he is finished. So take advantage of this situation by reminding the receiver from time to time that you are indeed real, alive, well, and camping on the net, looking down his throat. Move! That is all it takes. One little head movement, foot movement, or racket movement will do the trick.

If you are not satisfied with these tactics, and indeed you should not be, prepare your attack in earnest. You have everything going for you. You know where your partner will serve and what the spin will do. You know where your partner will move to and how long it will take him to get there. You know where the majority of returns are likely to go. You know your own capabilities, what is expected of you, and where you will hit the ball if you poach to cut it off. You also know that even if you go for the poach and are unsuccessful, the attempt will remain in the receiver's mind. With all this in mind, you are not just a post out there, but an alive, aggressive adversary that will eat him up alive. POACH AT EVERY OPPORTUNITY. This is what happens to the receiver when he knows that you will poach: Distracted by your offensive threat to his return, he rushes his return or takes his eye off the ball, which results in a weak return or an error. As a result, he becomes demoralized at his failure to return well, and this adds to his inability to return. Things go from bad to worse. Feeling frustrated and threatened, he loses confidence and, finally, when he begins to feel responsible for his team's poor showing, he feels guilty and his play goes from bad to worse. The result is obvious.

But if your opponent happens to be wiser than the average bear and is not given to such easy frustration and despair, he may use your poaching to your disadvantage. Be careful; those guys over there are not to be trusted. He may lob over you or hit down your line after you have left home to go poaching. You must be on your toes and develop a fine sense of anticipation and timing. Watch the receiver's body position to see if he is balanced, and observe the angle of his racket head. These are the things you should work on in practice so that you can rely on reflex in a match. Doubles is a reflex game, with more reflex involved than in singles, so you must learn the game so well that you don't need to think about it when you're in a match. After a while it will become automatic.

When you leave your position for the poach, keep in mind that you are going to hit the ball at the feet of the opposing netman. Even if your shot is weak, he will still have to hit the ball up, and by that time both you and your partner will be standing on top of the net.

If you begin to go for the shot, finish it off. If you have gone across the center service line to cut off a slow return, you should stay in the half of the court you entered. Your partner, seeing that you have made the move, should quickly switch to cover the court you vacated, keeping the triangle in effect.

Some tactics to use on the receiver are the fake and the Australian, or tandem, formation, also known as the "I" formation. The fake is simple. Just as the receiver is about to hit the ball, shift your weight or move your head in the direction of the center of the court but hold your position for the shot. Especially if you have been poaching successfully, a fake is likely to draw the ball toward you for an easy winning volley. Or it may result in a weak return or an outright error. In any case, by faking you have become a moving foreign object in the receiver's eye, and he must not disregard you.

The formation called the tandem, or "I," is used when the receiver has been expert in his crosscourt return of service. Nothing you have done has deterred him from his lovely returns. He is grooved and, as far as he is concerned, you may as well not be on the court.

The next time your partner serves to this master of service returns, take a position about the same distance from the net as

25

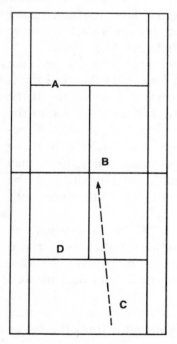

C tries the middle of the court on the return of serve, but B steps in quickly to cut it off. Player A continues toward the net. C follows in behind his return as D moves in.

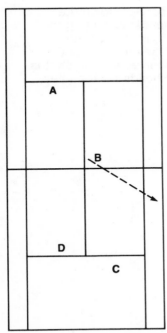

B volleys the ball sharply, angling it into the alley for a winner. Player A will finish the point near B. C and D have no chance for a play on the ball.

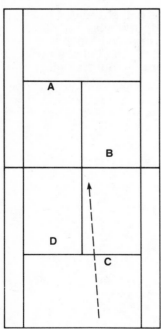

C returns service down the middle where B is waiting to knock it off. B steps in and angles the ball in front of D. Player A sees where the shot is going and heads for the alley.

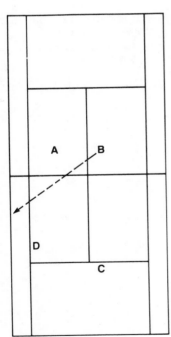

The ball is out of play as D makes a desperate try for it. C moves over to guard the middle in case D makes a return. A joins B in the triangle. This illustrates the point that even though you believe you have hit a winner, it is a good tennis strategy to move into the best offensive position after the shot.

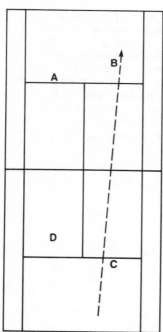

Player B goes back for the lob
as C and D close on the net. A
stops his forward motion and
starts back to join his partner.

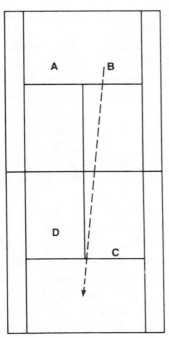

B smashes the overhead
between C and D for the winner.
A and B follow in behind the
shot. Note how player B keeps
his head up and his eyes on the
ball as he hits the overhead.

31

your usual position but one foot on the *other* side of the center service line. This puts you in the direct line of your partner's serve, so he must take up a service position as close as possible to the center of the court. If the receiver is fool enough to hit a crosscourt return to this alignment, you will be in the perfect spot to knock it off. But do not worry too much about this happening; the receiver will surely rise to the occasion and hit down the line. These down-the-line shots are the responsibility of the server, who now must cover the half court you normally occupy. The pressure is on the server, as he will have a more difficult volley than he would normally have. But the purpose of the tandem has been accomplished in that the rhythm of the fine receiver who has been making both you and your partner miserable has been broken. This technique should only be used when everything else has been tried and has failed.

What about lobs over your head on the service return? They are your responsibility, and you *must* run them down. Take them on the fly if possible, so that you can maintain your offensive position near the net. Your partner will be charging the net after his serve and will not be able to change direction to cover your court. If you must take the ball off the ground, then give it your best shot and set up the triangle on the baseline. Your best shot in this situation is the lob. If it is effective, the court position of the teams will be reversed. You and your partner will be at the net, and the opposition will be on the defense at the baseline. This can result in a lobbing duel that will probably end only when one of you throws up a short lob that is then taken on the fly and smashed for a winner. Be sure your lobs are high and deep.

After the return of service, *all* lobs down the middle are to be taken by the man with the best overhead. Agree on this between yourselves before the match to avoid confusion during play. If there is ever any confusion or hesitation, sing out "Mine" or "Yours" as appropriate according to the previously made decision. If for any reason the best smasher cannot take the shot, it is up to him to call out "Yours." One word will do it. For Pete's sake, no sentences such as "You take it" or "Hey, I'm sorry, but

offensive

I'm wrong footed; would you be so kind?" One quick, sharp command is sufficient; use it.

Finally, there are times when signals must be used between the netman and the server to indicate whether or not you, as netman, are going to cross or stay. The only signal that is needed is an open or closed hand behind your back to clue your partner. Once the signal has been given, you are absolutely committed. If you say you are going, you *must* go. If you say you are staying, let nothing drag you from your position.

Remember that you and your partner must function as one mind, finely tuned to each other for the best possible results. This comes with hours and hours of hard work on the tennis court. As the netman you are in the best possible position for the kill, so practice your volley assiduously. Your dedication in practice will emerge when it counts. This develops your partner's confidence in you, and when all is said and done, this may be the most important point of all.

THE WHOLE THING ONE MORE TIME:

1. Choose your partner carefully.
2. Be kind to your partner.
3. Your partner's game should complement your own.
4. Work together as a team.
5. The stronger player plays the backhand side.
6. Your net position is six to eight feet from the net and half the distance between the center service line and the inside alley line.
7. Be ready.
8. Remind the receiver of your presence—move.
9. Poach at every opportunity.
10. Errors and weak returns result from poaching.
11. The receiver will hit crosscourt, down your line, at you, or he will lob.
12. Watch the receiver's racket for clues.
13. Anticipate.

33

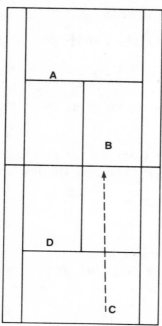

B has been waiting all day for this one. C returns the serve high down the middle, directly at B. Player A continues toward the net. D starts toward the center of the court.

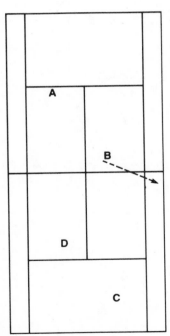

B steps in and drops the ball
just over the net into the alley. A
keeps coming and will be next
to B at the net, in preparation
for a possible return. A's
preparation is important,
especially after the chancy drop
shot.

14. Hit the ball at the netman's feet.
15. Get back into position quickly.
16. Stay when you have crossed the center line.
17. Maintain the triangle.
18. Fake.
19. Use the tandem when all else fails.
20. Run down all lobs over your head on your side of the court.
21. All lobs down the middle are to be taken by the player with the best overhead.
22. Use one-word commands when necessary.
23. Use hand signals when necessary.
24. Attack.

chapter three

receiving serve

Tennis instructors, teachers, professional coaches, and players all agree on the necessity for developing the many skills required to play the game of doubles. As players and students of the game we hear about the virtue of keeping the ball in play more than any other tenet of the game. There is no doubt about the importance of this basic premise, but beyond this there is much dispute about which skill contributes most to winning doubles.

Some maintain that the volley is of prime importance, with emphasis placed on getting close to the net and hitting down on the ball to a spot deep and near the center of the court. Other teams concentrate on hitting the best percentage shot and playing the game as close to textbook perfection as possible. The poach has been emphasized as absolutely necessary for winning a partner's serve, and it is therefore an integral part of the tactics of those who emphasize the absolute necessity of holding serve.

There are those who emphasize communication, encouragement, and harmony between partners as the human skills to be developed for winning play, and, of course, no one debates their position. We also hear about "continuing a winning game" and "changing a losing game," the necessity of consistency, the need for power and touch, and the value of the smash.

We do not dispute the necessity for developing these skills in order to play the game well. But we would place any one of them second to the return of service.

Since we consider holding service to be vital to winning doubles, breaking serve naturally follows close behind. With highly skilled players, one service break is usually enough to win a set. The burden lies on the receiver of service, and he must be expert in his ability to return *consistently* and *effectively* if a break is to be achieved.

POSITION

As the receiver, take your position approximately one foot inside the inside alley line and on or just inside the baseline. Your depth will depend upon the power of the server.

TACTICS

In doubles it is important to take the ball as early as possible for the return, so take advantage of a weak serve and move in as close as possible. If you can take it on the rise, so much the better. If the server is blowing you off the court, then move farther back to give yourself a little more time. Some serves come in at over one hundred miles per hour, and this gives you less than a second to discover the best strategy and respond.

Assuming the server is giving you his best three-quarter-speed kicker, is dropping it into the corner near the center service line to your backhand, and is following it to the net, the minimum objective you must realize is: RETURN THE SERVICE. Even a weak return is better than none, since you cannot win a point without getting the ball over the net.

The best and most effective return is a medium-paced cross-court shot that lands at the feet of the oncoming server. You understand the thinking of the man at the net, so you can expect him to move toward the center of the court, thereby reducing the court area available for crosscourt returns. So your return must be fast enough and low enough to elude the efforts of the netman but slow enough to make the server hit off the ground, half volley, or volley from below the level of the net. The whole idea here is to put pressure on the server to make a good volley, give your netman a chance to poach, and bring you to the net behind your return. Your service return and follow-up to the net should place you on the offense and give you the best opportunity for winning the point.

When you are receiving a second serve, the odds have shifted in your favor. We recommend that you press this advantage by running around your backhand at every opportunity. This causes consternation on the part of the server, freezes the opposing netman, opens up the court for your shot, and enables you to hit an attacking shot with your forehand. Practice running around your backhand to familiarize yourself with the moves and the feeling. It is important that you feel comfortable and natural using this tactic. This radical move on your part does some interesting things to the mind of the server. Once you have nailed his second service down the middle for an outright winner, he will begin to think about getting his first serve in. That is exactly what you want him to do—think. Thinking affects the effectiveness of his first serve, causing him to continue to fault or to slow it down. When this happens, move in for the kill. Running around the backhand further works to your advantage by allowing your netman to move toward the center in order to poach. It also allows both of you to attack.

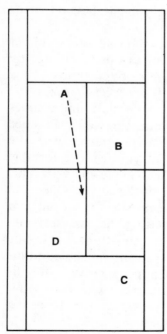

Player A takes the return of
serve well out in front but is
forced to volley from below the
net. C is closing quickly after
his return. B and D alter their
positions slightly as the play
develops.

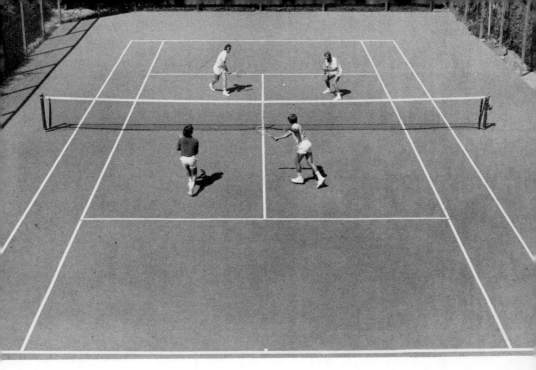

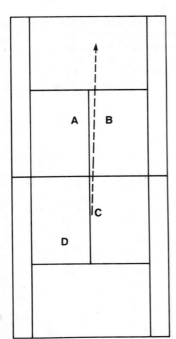

C hits down the middle with a perfect forehand drive volley. D moves in to complete the triangle.

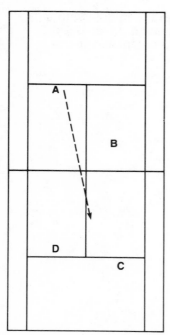

Player A lifts the return of serve
up from the service line as C
and D close in for the volley.

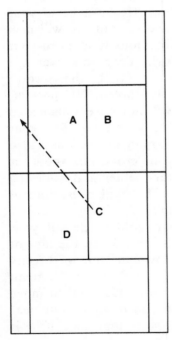

C volleys behind A as A moves to cover the middle. C and D are in the triangle and in the best offensive position.

Remember that doubles is a game of attack, so you should take advantage of every opportunity for getting to the net. That is where winning is.

Obviously, you are not always going to be able to traumatize the server and reduce him to little drops of perspiration on the court. You must then count on your skill and knowledge while applying the art of magic to your craft. As receiver, you must be somewhat of a magician in order to return effectively and consistently. Being consistent does little good if your consistency is being eaten up by the netman or battered to the baseline by a server volleying behind his serve. You must practice the art of concealment and learn to mask your moves and hide lobs up your sleeve. Let us emphasize that it is effective consistency that breaks service. This means that you must have at your command a variety of shots that you can put into effect at the last possible moment.

You must never forget that the netman awaits, while at the same time you dare not think about him. He must be in your mind without monopolizing it. With practice, your eye will pick up his moves and relay them without conscious thought to your racket. Using your magic, drop a high, deep lob over the netman's head and follow it to the net. If he has grown confident poaching, it may catch him flat-footed. His partner, the server, will be rushing the net and will not have a chance to recover in time to hit the overhead. This places you and your partner at the net on offense and in the triangle. The lob is also effective when the server is volleying your crosscourt shots for winners. If he is coming in hell-bent for leather and volleying well within the service court, lob him. That will cause him to pause and think it over. Get them to think!

There will be days when the netman gobbles up all your returns within reach and the server kills the rest. In the face of this, you might occasionally cane one down the line or directly at the netman. Remember that you must keep the netman honest. A winning shot down his alley may cause him to move over an inch or two, which will enable you to slide your next return just out of his reach crosscourt. More than that, if he is thinking about guarding his belly button, his mind is off the game and on survival. That is super. Put that thought in his head as well.

The object of the return of service is to put the server in the worst possible position. He, of course, wishes to get to the net and eat up your return. If it is possible for you to move in close, take the ball on the rise and hit wide in the alley. You will have executed the most effective return in the game. Taking the ball early gives you more time to get to the net to assume the triangle, and being in close allows you sharper angles and gives you more court to hit into, because the closer the server gets to the net, the less court you have available. Move in.

Keep in mind that about eighty-five percent of the serves will come to your backhand and only fifteen percent to the forehand side. Add to this your knowledge of (1) the server's best percentage serve, (2) where you are in the match, (3) the server's tendency to gamble, and (4) his psychological frame of mind, and you may find yourself inching closer to your backhand, tempting him to try a serve he does not really want to use. This maneuver at the right time may draw a fault or even a double fault. If the server doesn't gamble and go for the ace, you are still in good position for the return.

Always move in a step or two for the second serve. Second service aces are few and far between. The two steps are worth your gamble, and the attempted ace is not worth his. Your choices for a sharp return are greater on a second serve than on a first, and if you are in closer, you and your partner have a better opportunity to go to the net and take the offense. Every step closer to the net is to your advantage. Move in and take the serve and keep on going.

Four shots are available to you on the return of serve. They are the medium-paced (sliced or chopped) shot, low and cross-court; the topspin crosscourt drive; the flat/fast/drive, low and crosscourt, down the line or at the netman; and the lob (offensively or defensively over netman or server.).

Use the slow or medium-paced spinning crosscourt return most of the time. You want to put as much pressure on the

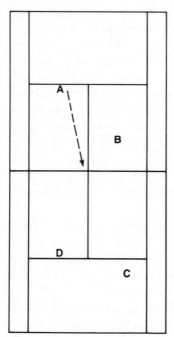

A volleys the return of serve low from midcourt as C and D take advantage of the low return to rush the net.

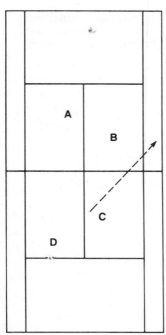

C moves in and takes the high volley early, angling it in front of B for a winner. Note that when a player is forced to hit the ball up, his opponent has the opportunity to hit it down.

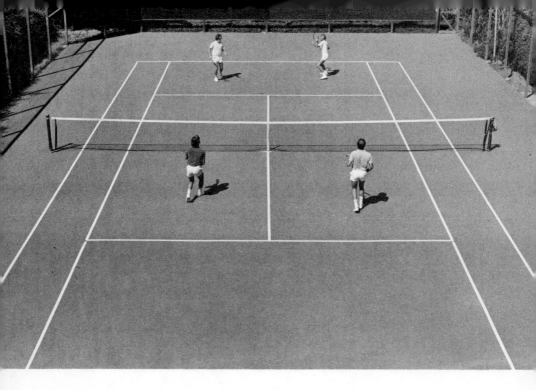

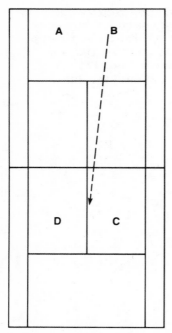

B lines up the service return lob as C and D take an offensive net position. A backpedals to join B.

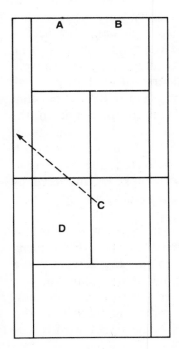

C anticipates the smash and cuts off the ball with a sharply angled backhand volley in front of A. A and B are left of the baseline. C and D follow the volley and set up the triangle.

server as possible, so you must make him work to capacity. Keep in mind that the server must serve, follow quickly toward the net, make his return, and move into position while your only physical activity is returning the serve and following in. As the match moves into the second or third set and the server has tired, the greater your advantage. When players are equal in ability, a match will sometimes be won by the team in better physical condition. The slow crosscourt return will force the server to volley up, in itself a difficult shot. If you also hit the shot with accuracy, you can have the server standing on his head, digging the ball out of the court, while your netman patiently waits for the ball to come up.

The topspin drive travels faster than the medium-paced return but also drops faster. This is an effective return, but since it is hit with more pace, it will come back at you more quickly, keeping you from getting as close to the net as you would like. Even though the ball is dropping and the server may have to volley it up, it still gives him an opportunity for a better volley than does the slower paced return. Also, you have sacrificed a precious step or two while allowing the opposing team to set up their triangle at the net. However, do not give up the topspin drive completely, for it belongs in your arsenal of shots and will have great effectiveness against different players. Remember that deception is the name of the game and you are the magician, the deceiver with the shot up his sleeve. If you have a variety of shots, your opponents will never know what to expect. Keep this in mind as well: After the server has delivered, the game is in your hands. Whatever you come up with must be answered by the other team. So take charge with your return, and give them something to respond to.

The flat drive is your big gun and is used against a weak first service. It may be hit higher over the net than the other returns because of its speed and can be used to pin the server to the baseline. When this occurs, the classic act of one man up, one man back is on, and if you have followed your drive to the net, you and your partner have established the triangle and have the best chance of winning the point. A fast, flat, deep return forces the server to play a difficult long volley, stop and hit off the ground, or half volley. Any one of the three is meat for the grinder. When you have hit his first serve with authority, he probably will not try it again for a while. However, when he does power one in, tee off and hit it down the line or at his netman. If it goes for a winner, olé. If the netman must pull fuzz from his navel, perhaps he will have a few choice words to say to his partner. Either way, the flat drive has its place in your bag of tricks.

We come now to a shot that gladdens our hearts and brings frowns to your opponents—the lob. We might go so far as to say that the players who can lob and lob effectively will strike terror in the hearts of their opponents. There is no better shot to break the rhythm of a team than a well-placed offensive lob. When the server is scoring winners with his serve and his partner is having a picnic at the net, sneak one of these little gems over his head, and see what happens. If you have been in a long match and find yourself in the third set, have a little conference with your partner and agree to throw up a few lobs. Do not forget that the most tiring of all strokes is the overhead, so even if your opponents decide to smash a few of your lobs, they may do more damage to themselves than to you. Also, in a long match that has been played fast and furiously, resulting in a tiring team, a decided change of pace just might swing the match in your favor by causing that all-important service break. Finally, if you find yourselves in trouble (and you will have those days when volleys go away and service returns are picked off like cherries from the tree), call your partner back to the baseline and lob everything in sight. It could cause a break in concentration on the part of the server and create a brand-new climate in the game. When desperate, try anything!

THE WHOLE THING ONE MORE TIME:

1. Keep the ball in play.
2. Volley down on the ball whenever possible.

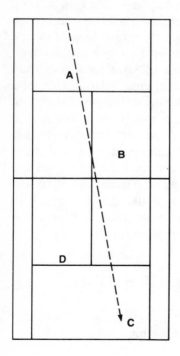

Player A serves to C, who takes
it on the rise as D starts to move
toward the middle of the court.

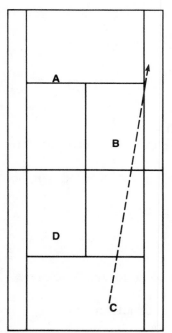

Getting into the shot, C drives
the ball down the line for a
winner. In case B can get his
racket on it, D is moving to
cover any possible return.

3. Play the best percentage shot.
4. Poach at every opportunity.
5. Hold your serve.
6. Communicate with your partner.
7. Keep a winning game; change a losing game.
8. Develop power and touch.
9. Be consistent.
10. RETURN THE SERVE.
11. The receiving position is approximately one foot inside the inside alley line and from the baseline to several feet inside the baseline, depending on the serve.
12. Take the ball as early as possible.
13. Return of service is a *must*!
14. The best return is a medium-paced, crosscourt shot to the middle of the court.
15. Keep crosscourt returns low over the net.
16. RUN AROUND YOUR BACKHAND ON ALL SECOND SERVES.
17. Follow your return to the net.
18. ATTACK!
19. Set up the triangle at the net.
20. Practice the art of concealment.
21. *Effective* consistency breaks service.
22. Develop a variety of returns.
23. If the netman is poaching successfully, lob.
24. Follow to the net all lobs that are over the heads of your opponents.
25. Keep the netman honest by hitting a flat drive down his alley or directly at him.
26. Taking the ball early or on the rise gives you:
    a. more court to hit into
    b. sharper angle possibilities
    c. more time to close
27. Eighty-five percent of all serves will come to your backhand.
28. Move in two steps for a second serve.
29. Every step toward the net increases your advantage.
30. Move in! Attack! Establish the triangle!

31. The four basic shots for return of service are:
    a. medium-paced
    b. topspin drive
    c. flat drive
    d. lob
32. The more a server is forced to serve, the greater the receiver's advantage.
33. Force the server to volley up.
34. Practice deception.
35. Hit the flat drive higher over the net and go for depth.
36. Lob to break the rhythm of the game and to disconcert the netman.
37. At the end of a long match no one wants to see a lob.
38. Lob when you are far behind or in any other kind of trouble.
39. Lob when absolutely desperate. Remember to attack the net with your partner behind any lob that goes over your opponents' heads.

chapter four

the defensive netman

It has been determined that the stronger player will play the odd court because of the advantages this side offers the receiving team. You will recall that most of the pressure points, including game points, are played on that side, and most returns are placed down the middle, to the forehand volley of the player covering that side.

POSITION

When the match begins, make sure that as the defensive netman you are in the best position to assist your partner and to make your presence known to the server.

Take your position one step inside the service line, halfway between the inside alley line and the center service line, facing the net. This places you in the best defensive position to guard a majority of the court in case of a weak return by your partner. If his return is less than perfect and the netman poaches, you may get a chance to make a play off his volley. If you were to play approximately the same position as the server's netman, you would not have a chance to make a play. That position, up close to the net, would open up the whole court behind you for the poacher to hit into. The closer you move to the net before your partner's return, the more vulnerable your position. The same holds true in retreating to the baseline. You can see that a position at or near the baseline opens up the court in front of you and renders you almost helpless. You cannot attack or defend well if the netman poaches. And if your partner returns safely, you are automatically on defense, with only an outside chance of gaining an offensive position.

TACTICS

It is imperative that you assume the correct position. Not only will you be in the most appropriate position for defending, but you will also be in the most strategic position to attack. As the receiving team you must attack in order to win. It is virtually impossible to win at doubles playing a defensive game. So assume the best position and be ready to attack after your partner returns. You must be exceptionally alert. Try to react to the action of your opponents, for example, the netman. When you see him move, react accordingly. If he moves to poach, be alert and prepare for a shot at your feet or at your hip. If he holds his position, shift your attention to the server. Depend on your instant reaction to a total situation picked up in that flashing panorama from partner to netman to server.

When you see that the ball will clear the netman, move toward the net quickly and be ready for the returning volley, half volley, or ground stroke. Players above the club level can

57

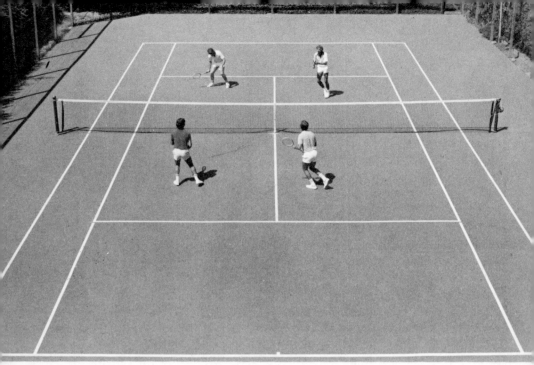

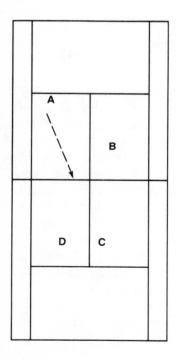

Player A half-volleys the excellent service return, popping it up over the center of the net. B moves to close off the middle.

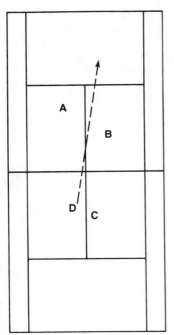

D steps in quickly to volley
down the middle for the winner.
C is in good position and is
prepared to volley with his
backhand.

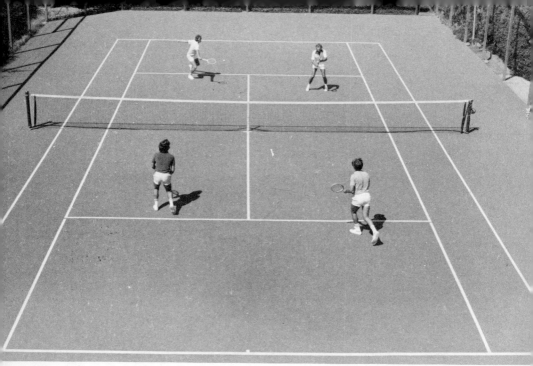

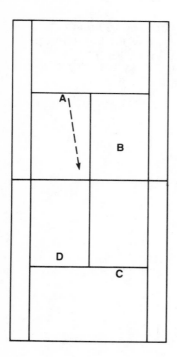

Player A is forced to volley the
return of service from near the
service line. Since he hits from
below the net, the ball gets up
too high to be effective.

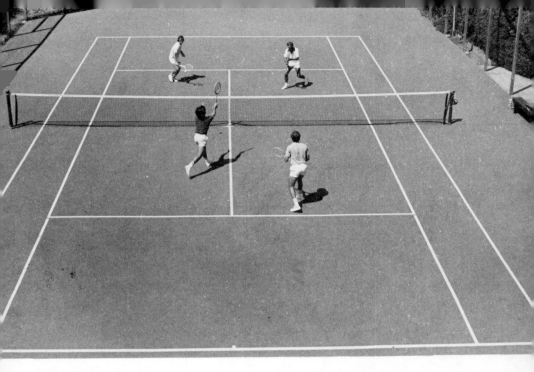

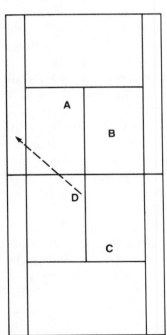

A and B move to guard the
center. C continues to improve
his position. D steps in and cuts
off the volley, hitting a sharply
angled crosscourt winner
behind A.

61

depend on this return being a volley, so we will focus on this shot. As the receiver's netman you must, absolutely must, guard your alley. Any ball hit safely there is an outright winner, and you may draw some static from your partner if you give away points in that way. To prepare, watch the server's body and racket position. You know that his best shot off the return of serve is deep down the middle and that most volleys will go there. You must move across and cut it off if possible. When you do, you instantly become the offensive team, with the best chance of winning the point. If you cannot reach the volley, hold your position and be ready for the ball after your partner's return. If you are formidable enough at the net, you can cause the server to lose concentration and falter on his volley. It is your job to cause him trouble. When you are certain that he cannot hit down your alley, move closer to the net and toward court center and force him to hit his volley wider than he would want. His wide volley causes the court to open up, offering a variety of possibilities to your teammate, who has followed in behind his return. If the server's volley is wide enough, your partner can take it on his strong forehand side and volley down the line, down at the netman's feet, or down the middle, as the best shot presents itself. You can force the server to volley wide by crowding the net or by faking or going all out for the poach. There is danger in going all out for the poach, for you will have left half the court exposed, and any shot back into it will go for a winner. Sometimes, when things are desperate, go ahead and gamble. At least you will plant the idea in the server's head that you can and will move. That will give him something to think about, and his having to consider one more obstacle is in your favor. Put as much into his head as you can.

What you really want the server to do is try a volley down your line, because the net is higher over the alley, and therefore a more difficult volley. If he can serve, rush the net, volley the ball over the highest point of the net and safely by you, then he deserves the point. All of the preceding problems are formidable, but perhaps the greatest problem the server has is in his head.

He knows that he must hit the ball well in order to win the point down the alley, and he knows that that is the very place you are prepared to defend. This is where the fake comes in. By faking a poach, you are inviting the server to hit his volley down your alley. However, you are there, ready for an interception and an almost certain winning volley.

The greater the pressure on the server, the greater chance you have of winning the points and eventually breaking serve. Crisp, low returns at the server's feet apply pressure, since he will have to volley up to you at the net. It is up to you to keep the pressure on him after the return of service. When you see that he is taking the ball low, anticipate the return and move to cut it off. Any movement on your part, whether you are faking or not, will be distracting. When you have applied enough pressure, notice how your ability to anticipate improves. The buildup of pressure caused by a succession of sharp service returns, where you have cut off his volleys, will eventually cause him to crack. If you have been quick and aggressive enough to force him to hit within your range, you may intimidate him into staying back after his serve and hitting off the ground. That is exactly what you want him to do. If this happens, you will have forced the serving team into the defensive, the most vulnerable position in doubles.

When the server fails to follow in behind his serve, his next shot will more than likely be a low drive or topped drive over the center of the net. This is his best shot. If you and your partner have moved into position behind the service return, you are now in the triangle and in the best position to win the point.

There is an exception to the general rule of attacking the net. When your partner is having trouble returning service and you are getting shelled by the poacher at the net, it would be wise to join your partner at the baseline. This move definitely places you on defense, but it gives you a chance to return something, whereas at the net all you can get is killed.

Whenever your partner lobs the netman and the lob is short, it is his duty to notify you of the catastrophe. One word will do

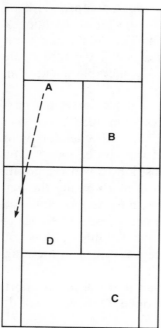

C's return of service is picked up wide by A, who has come in smartly behind his serve. The alley looks open, so he goes for it.

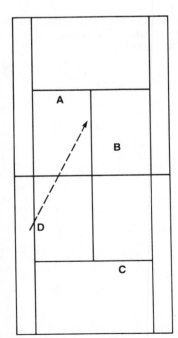

D moves in and drives the backhand volley between A and B for an outright winner, illustrating the point that you can get killed trying the netman's alley.

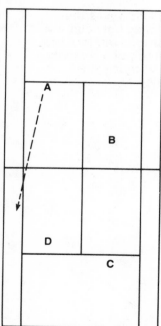

Player A decides to try it again.
He lifts the return of service up
and goes for the alley.

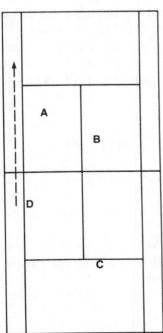

Sure enough, D steps across
and nails the return down the
line exactly as he should, while
A and B close off the middle. C
continues toward the net.

it. Calling "back" or "short" will send the message swiftly and clearly, and you must react just as quickly. Get out of the middle of the court (no-man's-land) and back to the baseline. Run backward, never taking your eye off the ball. Many a point has been lost by a player turning around and running for the baseline, only to be hit by the ball. It is embarrassing, too.

There is one more tactic you can use to disconcert the server. Alter your position at the service line by crowding the center service line. Use this tactic on second serves. Be alert, because if the server hits you with the ball, you lose the point. On the other hand, when you move to this position, the appearance of the court is drastically changed for the server. From where he stands, it appears as though the service area is much smaller. This may have a decided psychological effect on the server: Since he thinks he has less area to hit into, a fault or double fault may result.

Some of the tactics mentioned here are to be used only when you are in deep trouble. In general, we recommend textbook play and high percentage shots, using your skill and knowledge. Your game should be geared for the usual, but it goes without saying that you must be prepared for the unexpected. Sometimes you must create the unexpected, and in order to do so you must mix your skill with imagination.

THE WHOLE THING ONE MORE TIME:

1. The stronger player should play the odd court.
2. The return of serve sets the stage.
3. The defensive netman must make his presence known to the server.
4. The defensive netman's position is one step inside the service line, halfway between the inside alley line and the center service line, facing the opposing netman.
5. Being too close to the net before the return of service opens

up the back court; being too far back opens the forecourt.

6. Correct position affords the best defensive position as well as the most strategic position for attack.
7. You must attack to win.
8. Move when the opposition commits itself.
9. Guard your alley.
10. Cut off the volley and take the offense.
11. When you force the server to volley wide, your partner gets to pick his shot.
12. Poach, fake, and move.
13. Draw the down-the-line volley.
14. Make the server aware of your presence.
15. Anticipate.
16. Pressure the server at every opportunity.
17. Take all middle-of-the-court volleys.
18. Establish the triangle.
19. Take all lobs over your head and down the middle.
20. If you must lob, make sure you have called your partner to your side.
21. Move together wherever you go.
22. Agree on which shots belong to whom before the match.
23. Move back to your partner's side if you are getting shelled after your partner's return.
24. It is your partner's duty to notify you by a one-word command in case of a short lob.
25. Run backward when retreating, and never take your eye off the ball.
26. Move closer to the center service line to disconcert the server.
27. Play textbook doubles and high percentage shots.
28. Use your imagination.
29. Develop instinct, quickness, fleetness, courage, meanness, and fakery.
30. Establish the triangle.
31. Attack.

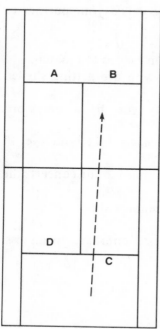

B moves back to take the service return lob. Player A backpedals to join B. C and D rush to the net as B hits the overhead.

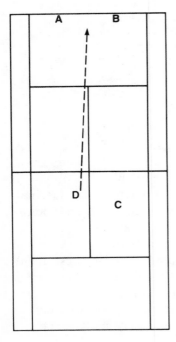

As the ball clears the net, D attacks and volleys the return up the middle, directly between A and B. A and B are in good defensive positions. C and D set up the triangle.

chapter five

mixed doubles

While doubles is a distinctly different game from singles tennis, mixed doubles is like no other game in the world. There are as many approaches to the game as there are people who play it. It is obvious that we cannot cover every approach to this fascinating game, so we decided to agree on a couple of things before giving you a personalized view into its machinations.

First, we assume that the best male player in the world would beat the best female. Second, we assume that the best men's doubles team would defeat the best women's team. We further assume, in top professional play, that the man will always be the stronger of the two and will be expected to play as much as seventy percent of the court and play as many balls as he can reach. Finally, we assume that most play will be directed toward the female in adherence to the following doubles maxim: "Intimidate the weaker player."

Earlier we talked about the importance of choosing a partner who is totally compatible both in skill and emotion. Such compatibility is even more important when choosing a partner for mixed doubles. Since the man is the stronger player, it is his place to hold a tight rein on his emotions and to bolster and encourage his partner at all times. He must understand the tremendous pressure that is on her and never admonish her for an error. He must understand her temperament as well as her capabilities and be ready to back her up, win or lose. He must also understand the importance of listening to what she has to say, and he should encourage her to talk it up. It is the man's job to bring his partner from the pits of despair and guilt that come so easily after ball after ball has been slammed at her and past her and lobbed over her. He is not allowed a grimace, a shrug, a dirty look, a dropped racket, or any other obvious display of negative emotion. His is not to reason why; his is but to offer a kind word and to resolve to hit better shots.

The female should be a tower of strength when her partner errs and when the chips are down. There is no other sport in the world that has a greater potential for tearing even a great team apart than mixed doubles. So pick the right partner, get it together, and keep it that way.

STRATEGY

While each of us will discuss the mixed doubles game from a personal point of view, we hope that both tactics and psychology will emerge. Cynthia will present the woman's side and Peter the man's.

—Cynthia:

I always take the even court in mixed doubles. Pressure points almost always occur during play originating in the odd court, and the stronger player must assume that responsibility. Also, the odd court gives the man the middle of the court from which

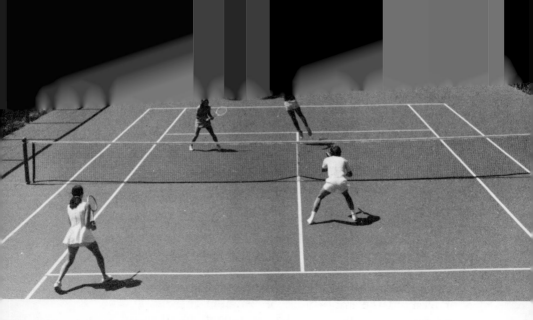

"The odd court gives the man the middle of the court from which to volley, as well as the best position to hit his overhead."

to volley as well as the best position to hit his overhead. When I win a point in the even court, we are in a better position psychologically to win the next point. If I lose a point, the man can even things up.

I usually play a little farther back for the man's first serve and move in a step or two for his second. My plan is to play the woman. I realize that I am not strong enough to outhit the man and that his superior speed will get him to the net for a winning volley or a placement that keeps me on defense. I must use my brains and skill to try to outwit my opponents. So I think "woman" and concentrate on making her hit as many balls as I can. When she constantly has to make a play, the pressure builds. If we can get her to crack, we will win the match. Sure, she is expecting me to play her, but she does not know what shot to expect. She is relying on her partner's first serve, which I will lob most of the time; but if I get a chance at a second serve, I am going to lob, hit right at her, or try her alley. If I can get her to hit a weak return, I know my partner is there waiting to eat it up. If he gets the play, I know he will hit it in the woman's direction, and if I take her return, she will be my target, too. If I

"My plan is to play the woman."

ever get a chance to really hit one of my male opponent's second serves, I will cane it right at the woman.

When I am serving, I expect my partner to poach like wild when I serve to the woman. I will try to put my best spinning first serve to her backhand. When my partner is successful in cutting off her return, she begins to think about his presence. If he has continued success poaching or smashing her lobs back at her, she will become unnerved and psyched out and grow more tentative on her returns, which will only increase her failure.

If she is successful in getting her return past my partner, I will almost always volley right back to her. My partner knows where my volley is going and is prepared for her return. Sometimes when her return is wide and high, I move in and volley it down at the feet of the man or, in case he moves to intercept my volley, hit behind him. When I must continually volley the return of service, I will try the netman's alley once in a while to keep him honest.

When I serve to the man, I slow my first serve down and put a great deal more spin on the ball in order to bring it in. I cannot overemphasize the importance of getting the first serve

"If he gets the play, I know he will hit it in the woman's direction."

"When I am serving, I expect my partner to poach like wild when I serve to the woman."

"When I get the volley, I will hit directly to the woman."

in, especially to the man. A first serve in play allows my partner the opportunity of poaching, whereas he can only guard his area when I must serve a second ball. When I volley behind my first serve, I again concentrate on the woman, hitting my volley directly at her or low to either side. Both my partner and I will be at the net, waiting for her return. When I throw in a second serve to the man, I know he will run around his backhand and cane one straight at me. My only defenses against this are a quick reflexive move that will get the ball back somewhere in the court.

My time of greatest concentration is when the woman is serving. This is the time to go for the service break. The pressure is on her to hold, and she must face my partner at the net when I return and again when serving to him. It is my job to set up the play by hitting the ball straight back to her. She must contend with the ball, my partner, and me. If I can get the ball safely by the netman, the odds are evened, and anybody can win the point. I may try the netman's alley once in awhile, just to remind him that he must stay pretty close to home. When the netman is knocking off my returns or the woman is getting in

77

"When the woman is getting in close and volleying well, I will throw up a lob over her head."

"When my partner is serving, I prepare for every return."

close and volleying well, I will throw up a lob over her head. I never lob the man if I can help it, but if I can lob over the woman's head as she comes charging in, she will have to stop and go back. If she lets it bounce, my partner and I are both on top of the net, waiting to volley.

I always prepare to run around the woman's second serve and take it with my forehand. The netman is frozen by this maneuver, and the majority of the court becomes the woman's responsibility. She will have to make a super volley to stay in the point.

When my partner is serving, I prepare for every return. I know that our opponents' attack will be the same as ours would be and that I am going to be the target for both players. When my partner serves to the woman, I get ready for a lob or a shot directly at me. Either way, I am going to hit back to the woman. When I can poach, I will hit back deep to the woman or, if I catch the netman out of position, go for the winner.

—Peter:

There is a great deal more strategy involved in mixed doubles than either singles or men's doubles, and it is a far more complicated game to play. I know I will have to play more of the court, and this changes all thought and reflex patterns developed in playing the other two games.

In men's doubles the vulnerable area of the court is down the middle, but in mixed doubles it is the woman's side, so rather than hitting a ball crosscourt I must now change my strategy in consideration of the woman's position. This is a whole new game, and I find I must concentrate harder in order to play the game well.

My point of concentration is on the woman. Cynthia made the same point, but I want to reemphasize that both of us will have a single focus point, and it will always be the woman. I am personally going to intimidate her like crazy. Any time I can cane one close to her, I will. I want her to know that she will have to fight for her life if she stays at the net. I want her out of

"When I can poach, I will go for the winner or hit down on the woman."

"The geographical vulnerability of the court changes from down the middle to the woman's side."

"I want to re-emphasize that both of us will have a single focus point, and it will always be the woman."

there and on the baseline. I am not going to slam one directly at her or try to hurt her. That would be too easy, and, besides, it is not worthy of the man. If I can scare her out, we get the net and the win. No hard feelings, you understand. That's just the name of the game.

When I serve to the woman, I never let her see two balls the same. It is my intention to cause her as much confusion as I can, because I don't want her to be able to anticipate a serve and then cream my partner. I try to put as much spin and kick into my serve as I can in order to destroy her confidence. I want her to hit the ball back to me, and when she does, I will volley directly back to her, putting as much "extra" on it as possible to cause her problems. If she lobs my partner, I set up the triangle and we attack together behind the overhead. All the rest of the time I will be crowding the center of the court, making as many plays as I can.

I always serve very tight to the man, making sure I get my first serve in. Anything he returns that I can volley will go to either side of the woman at the net or directly at her. Let me point out that volleying directly at the woman at the net is not

"I want her to hit the ball back to me, and when she does, I will volley directly to her . . . "

"I will be crowding the middle of the court making as many plays as I can."

82

"I always follow my return to the net, and if I get the ball, I will volley to either side of the woman or go down the middle."

Although the man might be playing all over the court, winning a mixed doubles match depends upon the *woman's* resilience—her ability to respond with strategic and psychological strength to the mixed doubles tactics.

the same as lining up a cane to take off her head. Besides, she knows that she is vulnerable, and she expects the shot. If the man lobs my partner off my serve, it is my responsibility to cover it and all other lobs over my partner's head. When I shift to her court for the smash, she switches, sets up the triangle, and we play it from there.

When my partner is serving, I am all over the net like a rash. I want the return from either opponent, and I will intimidate both of them to get it. It is my purpose to cut off as many balls as I can and to leave only those my partner can handle easily. I do not want to leave her much court to protect or have her hit too many returns.

When receiving the woman's first serve, I always hit a medium-paced return and follow it directly to the net for the volley. If she serves up a second serve, I automatically run around my backhand and drive the ball right back to her. I do not worry about the netman, because he has no place to go. He is glued to the spot, and if he does move, I will hit behind him for a winner.

My strategy when receiving the man's serve is relatively simple. I know that if I lob, he will go back for it and have the opportunity to win the point on his smash. If I hit near the woman at the net, she could hit for my partner's feet or go for the winner down the middle. That leaves a soft, medium-paced return to the center of the man's court that will force him to volley up to me or my partner. I want to avoid the big return that gives the server the opportunity to attack my partner.

I always follow my return to the net, and if I get the ball, I will volley to either side of the woman or go down the middle.

Even though we have assumed that the man will be the stronger of the two and will play most of the court and take most of the balls, it is important that the reader understand one final point: Although the man will be playing all over the court, *winning a mixed doubles match depends upon the* woman *hitting the right shot at the right time.*

chapter six

lefties

No matter what you have heard about left-handed tennis players, it is probably true. They convey a certain mystique, and to most right-handed tennis players they are a complete enigma. Actually, whether a lefty confuses your game depends upon your point of view. Are you going to play with one? Or against one? See what we mean?

PLAYING AGAINST A LEFTY

When you play against a lefty in doubles, you will notice some interesting things. First of all, he will usually, if not always, play the odd side, with his backhand covering the middle of the court. Tennis historians acknowledge that lefties usually have outstanding forehands but suffer somewhat on the other side. Their backhands, which may be steady, will usually be slower paced and easier to read. Lefties seem to have a problem hitting down the line with their backhands, which relieves the server's netman of some concern regarding his alley. Thus the netman is free to crowd the lefty on his return of service, forcing him to lob or attempt a difficult angle. The defensive netman should be prepared to poach on every first serve to the lefty's backhand and poach or fake on every second service to his backhand.

Because the lefty is in the minority, he will have a history of playing right-handers and, more than likely, will have been taught to play by a right-handed teacher. He has been trained to hit his forehand crosscourt to the backhand of his opponent, and his backhand will usually go there as well. He has become a natural "hit to backhand" player, and most of his rhythm and motion are so directed. This knowledge makes him somewhat predictable, especially in doubles. Because he has been grooved to hit crosscourt with his forehand, when he does go down the line, his accuracy suffers. The server knows he will be taking most of the lefty's returns with his backhand, and he should place his volley down the middle, the most vulnerable point.

The tandem is an excellent tactic to use against a left-hander who is effectively returning crosscourt. This strategy enables the server to serve directly over the lowest point of the net to the lefty's backhand. It also allows the server's netman to stand directly in the pathway of the lefty's favorite shot, and it forces the receiver to hit a backhand down the line, a vulnerable shot. When he hits this shot, both the netman and the server have the opportunity to volley with their forehands. Whatever the return, your answering volley should go down the middle unless one or the other of the receiving team is out of position; then go for the hole.

Lefties will sometimes attack behind a backhand lob return of serve, so if you are in the tandem, make sure it is agreed who will take the overhead. In the "I" formation, misunderstandings about overheads may result in chaos and collisions.

There is nothing that can disconcert a receiver so much as a lefty's fast, spinning serve going in the "wrong" direction. The lefty serves naturally to the backhand in both courts, pulling the even court receiver into the middle of the court and taking the odd court receiver wide and out of position. The player on the even side will have trouble following his backhand return to the net, since he will be moving laterally in order to make the return. His lateral move opens up the court, and the server's netman can volley to the open court for the winner. In order to head off this situation, the receiver should move about one foot to the left of his normal receiving position so that when the ball comes to his backhand, he won't have to scramble wide for the return, leaving a hole for the netman. He should also move in quickly and take the serve as early as possible. This is an offensive move that gets the ball in play before it can swing away and also allows the receiver to follow the return to the net.

A final point to remember is that the lefty's netman is going to hog as much of the net as he can get, and the odds are in his favor. Lob him as often as necessary to break his rhythm, confidence, and greed.

PLAYING WITH A LEFTY

Things are ever so much more rosy when you play with a lefty. The best part is that you do not have to play against him, those other guys do. You also have the advantage of understanding their problems. When your lefty unleashes his wide, swinging serve, you are at the net in "poacher's paradise." Ah, the pressure you can apply. Knowing his serve will be swinging wide to your opponent's backhand, you can cover the net like a rash, volleying down the middle and smashing overheads. You have the advantage at the net and the psychological advantage. You are in the best position to win your partner's serve. Keep a cool head, take your time, and go for winners. You will never have a better opportunity. When your lefty serves from the even court, keep in mind that both his forehand and yours are in the middle. When he serves from the odd court, the reverse is true. Be sure that you and he have agreed on who is to take down-the-middle shots. They should always be taken by the player with the stronger forehand or backhand volley.

PLAYING AS A LEFTY

When you are the lefty on the court, you have a distinct advantage. You have spent your tennis life playing right-handers, and they have spent their tennis lives avoiding you. This knowledge gives you a psychological edge that is hard to overcome. You are going to play the way you usually play, and they are going to have to turn their heads completely around to meet your left-handed game. When a left-hander is in the match, it is a completely different ball game. Use your left-handedness to every advantage. Keep your opponents guessing. Remember, you have the edge from the beginning. Keep it!

You should always take the odd court, even if your partner is the stronger player. It is your natural side and, more than likely, the one you grew up on. Both your forehand and backhand are grooved to hit to your opponent's backhand, and the odd court makes best use of this advantage. In general, return crosscourt as often as you can. When your opponents set up the tandem, hit a medium-paced backhand down the line and follow it in. The server will be forced to move to his right and toward the net to make the volley. If you have hit it well, your shot will either force him wider than he wants to go or will catch him moving across the ball, forcing him to hit off balance. Force your opponents to play your game. Your strength lies in the fact that their reflexes were developed against other right-handers. Take advantage of any momentary lapse that could break their timing and concentration.

Like any other player, run around a second serve and whip the ball crosscourt to the server's backhand. With the ball moving away from him and down, your opponent's return volley should leave something to be desired.

Do not be too concerned that the server will try to ace you on your forehand side. To do this, he must contend with a higher part of the net as well as your forehand. It is a difficult shot for him to hit, and he probably will not try it too often. Knowing this, you and your partner can crowd the center. Your partner should move near the center service line, and you should alter your position one step to your right. This position leaves a serving space that looks about the size of a postage stamp. Problems, problems. If the serve goes to your left, your forehand must be reckoned with. If he serves to your right, a fault is a distinct possibility. This alignment is a good tactic and should be used when you are in a bind.

When you are serving, use your wide swinging serve. It will be ten times more effective than your cannonball. While the cannonball is fast, it is also straight, and a good receiver can stand still and power it right back at you. The wide swinging serve forces the receiver to move, and when he does, he opens holes all over the court, setting up your partner for winning volleys.

Always serve to the backhand unless your opponent has altered his position so radically that a three-quarter-speed serve to his forehand will go for an ace. When you serve wide from the odd court, your netman can move over to his right to take shots that are forced there by your serve.

Keep in mind that as the receiver watches you serve, he is looking at a toss and delivery that is almost completely foreign to him. The receiver knows that he must move wide to hit the return and that his court will be exposed when he does. He knows that he must pass the netman or the point is lost immediately. He knows that he must get to the net, and he knows that that is almost impossible. So even before you hit your serve, the pressure on your opponents is tremendous. Applying your knowledge and skill can turn this pressure into disaster for your opponents.

All in all, the lefty adds variety to the already complicated game of doubles, and his presence on the court ensures a new dimension of play.

There is a lot to be said about left-handed tennis players, and right-handers have said it all.

chapter seven

seniors

If you are a senior who wants to take up doubles or resume play after some time away from the game, the first step is to get in shape. Use some of the exercises suggested in this book. Get into the best physical condition possible. You must not try playing yourself into shape, especially if you are going to play tournaments. Tennis is a strenuous game and even walking around on a court can take your wind. See your physician and get checked out.

A seasoned senior tournament player once remarked, "The net is still where the game of doubles is played, but these old codgers are getting so good at lobbing that it hardly makes coming to the net behind your serve worthwhile." He is right.

Even though the game is the same unless you are in the Masters class, to serve and volley is sometimes just not worth it.

Play the game according to this text, but if your serve has slowed down over the years or too much good food has taken its toll, take the return of serve off the ground and work your way to the net. The odds are that the receiver has not followed his return to the net, so hit back at him and come on in. Here is where you are most likely to encounter the lob, and if it comes, both you and your partner should retreat to the baseline and wait there until your opponents give you the opportunity to move back to the net. Work together and avoid one man up and one man back.

Senior doubles is a meticulous game that demands great skill and brilliant tactics to develop a point, making ball control essential and placement all-important. Seniors should set up their partner for the kill unless a weak shot is hanging on top of the net, waiting for the coup de grace.

Practice hitting overheads and throwing up lobs. Many seniors would rather run a ball down than hit an overhead, but this is a mistake. Be a hitter. Cut off the ball even if all you can manage is a defensive smash, so that you can maintain your aggressive position. If you let the ball bounce, you may find yourself defending the baseline.

The best advice we can give is to work on the serve, return of serve, and basic ground strokes. Doubles is a fundamental game, and unless you own the basic fundamentals, you will not be satisfied with your play. We realize that many seniors only have time to play weekend tennis, but if you are going to enjoy the game to the fullest, you must have the basic strokes down pat.

Be sure you are in good physical condition, see your physician, work on the basic strokes, and, above all, enjoy yourself!

chapter eight

juniors

Many juniors play the game of doubles as though there were four people on the court playing singles. The tendency is to go for the kill too soon and too often.

Let us emphasize the importance of developing patience while perfecting the control that is so necessary for good doubles play. The fruit of patience is winning, and for one player on a team to try winning by himself is absurd. Your partner is your greatest asset, and it is essential that you play with him and for him. Taking care of the ball and setting up the point for your partner is fundamental.

Overhitting and going for the outright winner is also characteristic of junior doubles. Doubles is a game of patience and placement. When the ball has been placed in the right spot, the return will beg for the kill. Play for the placement.

One must not forget that doubles is a team sport and should be played in rhythm. When the rhythm is good, so is the play. Rhythm is achieved when partners are in harmony, so choose a partner who complements your personality, emotions, style, and ability.

Play both sides of the court in practice to develop a complete understanding of the game and to determine which side each is to play. One day you might have to change your normal playing court, and when you do, unless you have practiced playing both courts, you will find that the view is different inside your head and on the court. Angles are different and require different strokes. Players are standing in different places. Movement is different, and choice of middle shots is confusing. It is important that you learn to play both sides, even though you should concentrate on one. There is the added benefit that when each player on the team learns to appreciate the position his partner plays, much is accomplished in developing teamwork and understanding.

Practice playing the game as it should be played. Sure, it is a lot of fun to grab just any old player and challenge the world, but your game will not improve that way. It is important that you learn to serve and volley just as the professionals do. The game they play is the same game you are playing. The only difference is skill.

Always make sure that you are in the correct position on the court. It is easy to get lazy and get caught in no-man's-land. Remember that you are part of a team, and you owe your partner the best you have to give.

You want the necessary skills to be automatic when you are in a match. So when you practice, serve and volley, poach, run down your own overheads, be patient, take care of the ball, make placements, run around all second serves to your backhand, follow service returns to the net, and, above all, encourage, support, complement, and protect your partner.

chapter nine

the elements

THE SUN

Old Sol is a fickle orb, bestowing his favors first on one team and then on the other. He is a capricious god, waiting behind the clouds for the moment of your match-ending overhead to sneak out and glare into your eye. He is powerful and demanding, slowly taking your strength and causing spots of darkness and flashes of light to appear inside your brain. He will be the cause of your delight and the object of your curses. Study him. Be aware of his wily ways and use your practice sessions to learn to deal with him.

It is the wise doubles team that has put in its time while the sun is high, determining how each member is affected by its glare. A thorough understanding of your capabilities will alleviate a great deal of conversation and strain when it comes time to decide side or serve at the spin of the racket.

When you win the spin, always elect to serve first. No doubt you will be given the sunny side and this is where your practice and knowledge pays off. As you know, it is extremely important to win the first game of doubles, so the man most competent in the sun should serve. Let us point out that this server may not be the best server of the two, but if the sun is or is going to be a factor, the one best suited to the sun should serve first. This adds to the responsibility of the server's partner, but if he is the stronger player, he is exactly where he should be.

If you lose the spin and your opponents elect to serve, do unto them as they would have done unto you. Give them the sun! This means that you have chosen the shady side from which to receive, but it also means that you too will have to contend with old Sol during your first serve.

When you receive, full concentration must be given to breaking serve. Sol is on your side, and he is a welcome partner. With his help and your expertise, you are in the best position for breaking serve. When the server tosses up the ball, he must contend with the glare or perhaps take a direct hit in the eye. Either way, he will be momentarily affected, and it is that instant that helps to shape the odds in your favor. If the server happens to catch one little ray, there will be a fraction of a second in which his vision is impaired. He could lose sight of the ball, and if he does, the point is yours.

All good players realize that the sun will sometimes be an obstacle to serving and that in order to compensate for its presence, some modification may be necessary in order to execute the best possible serve. This modification is usually in the toss or in a slight shift of stance. Whether you win or lose the toss, you will face the same situation when it is your turn to serve, and this is why you should pay your practice dues to the sun. You should develop a serve that is modified to alleviate the problem of the sun and is comfortable for you. The knowledge that you have such a serve will ease your mind and enhance your game.

When you find that your opponents have problems with the

sun, add to their discomfort by throwing up a few lobs. This is a delightful weapon to use, because when the sun is right the ball is difficult to take on the fly, and if your opponents let it bounce, you have a good chance of taking the net and the point. The best shots available to a player who has let a lob bounce are the overhead, the lob down the middle, and the topped drive low over the center of the net. Watch the hitter carefully and be ready for anything. If he has kept his eyes on the ball and the ball has passed through the sun, his return will probably be less than perfect.

Take advantage of the sun when he is your partner, and when he comes to the aid of your opponents, wear a hat.

HEAT

The sun may bother some players on some points, but the heat will get everybody. Here are a few tips for those who find themselves playing in Melbourne in January, in Fresno during the summer, or in Death Valley anytime.

If you are entered in a tournament and find that your starting time is anywhere between 11:00 A.M. and 2:00 P.M., find a nice cool spot and camp for a while before you play. It is not a bad idea to sit in the shade for an hour or so before your match. Walking around, especially in the sun, saps your energy and tends to make you listless. Even sitting in the sun will cause you to lose energy and become mentally and physically sluggish.

When you go on court, dress in whites, as colored clothing tends to absorb heat. Wear a headband to keep the sweat out of your eyes. It will act as an air conditioner, helping you keep a cool head. If you are prone to heavy perspiration, be sure to wear sweatbands to insure a solid grip on the racket.

While playing, it is extremely important to have towels, cold water, soda, and chairs at courtside. When you change courts, sit down in a chair and sponge your face and body with a towel saturated in cold water. Breathe deeply into the towel's coolness for comfort and oxygen from the water in the cloth. Drink small amounts of the soda for the sugar content and take glucose tablets to keep your body at its energetic best. Take your full rest time. There is no need to hurry. The heat will still be there when you get back on the court.

Playing the heat is much like playing the sun. Learn to use it. Everyone gets tired running when it is hot, so put the heat on your opponents and make them run. Alternate short shots with lobs. Keep the ball in play. Make your opponents hit extra shots. Keep cool.

COLD

It takes an act of Congress or a downpour to stop a tennis match, so be prepared to play in all kinds of weather. Extreme heat will take your strength, but the cold will penetrate your bones and make you long for an open fire and a hot cup of coffee. The cold can affect your enthusiasm as well as your body, so psyche yourself up and get ready to play.

Be sure to take your time warming up before the match. Put on plenty of clothes to avoid getting chilled. Find a spot to do some stretching and warm-up exercises, making certain that your body is loose on the inside and warm on the outside. Any or all of the exercises discussed in this book are recommended, and any that you have devised or found to be particularly good for you should be used. Do not do a halfway job of warming up. Do it right. The warm-up on the court prior to your match will not be sufficient, so the prematch warm-up is essential.

When you take the court in preparation for your match, keep your warm-up suit and sweaters on. If you find yourself restricted by your garments and unable to move about easily, take off some of the heavier items, but keep your warm-up suit on to hold in your body heat. If it is exceptionally cold, give some thought to playing with your suit on, but take it off if it hinders your play.

Keep in mind that the ball loses some of its life in the cold and must be hit harder to achieve the same efficiency it has in

97

warm weather. Even when hit harder, the ball will still stay down on the bounce, and you must be prepared to move forward and get down with it. Without a pregame warm-up, your legs will not want to move, and your knee joints will feel as though they are set in concrete.

When you find that you cannot pry your fingers from your racket handle and your touch is suffering from a lack of sensitivity; put on a light glove or a sweat sock with the toe cut out to warm up your hand. It does not do any good to suffer in silence out there in your summer outfit if you are getting killed. Take care of your body, and your game will take care of itself.

WIND

The wind is a tricky customer and must be treated with respect. It is fruitless to try ignoring it, because it will not go away. As with every other factor, you should learn as much as you can about the wind before you must play competitively in it. Practice with the wind at your back, in your face, crossing your court from either side; practice when it is gusty or swirling. The ball will behave differently in different weather conditions, so pay close attention to what you observe.

Most players do not like to play in the wind, so learn to love it and you will grab a psychological advantage by doing so. Big hitters are particularly disturbed when they find their normally blinding shots hanging on top of the net, looking the size of a basketball. When they change sides, the same shot will look like an aspirin fired from a cannon as it whizzes two inches above the net, straight into the back fence. In the wind your game will change drastically from one end of the court to the other. When playing against the wind, you can hit the ball harder without fearing that it will sail over the baseline, and you must, absolutely must, hit your lobs harder and higher for them to be effective. When the ball is hit too softly, the opposing netman will merely volley it for a winner or wait for it to bounce near the net before smashing it to any spot he chooses. High, deep lobs are particularly baffling and effective in the wind, and the opposition must be alert to play them well. Sometimes lobs will sail over the baseline, only to be blown back into the court. Never give up on a lob hit into the wind. Anything can happen to it. Just causing frustration on the part of your opponent is reason to throw up a few.

On the other hand, when the wind is at your back, you must be very careful with your lobs. Whereas you would hit for height and depth against the wind, with the wind at your back you must limit the height of the ball and allow the wind to carry it deep. When hitting downwind, take care of your ground strokes, keeping the ball low over the net. Take some of the speed off and use more spin for better control. You will have more time to hit off the ground, but the advantage you gain in time is countered by the erratic course taken by low bouncing balls. Be sure to get down with the ball and hit the percentage shot. Move in and volley as often as possible.

If you win the spin of racket, elect to serve. More than likely your opponents will choose to face the wind, and this choice offers you an interesting situation. Previously we talked about the importance of winning the first game and having the better server serve first, but with the wind at your back it is important that the weaker server serve first. The wind will assist his slower serve, making it more effective, and the netman's effectiveness will be increased. An added point in favor of this arrangement is that the stronger server will serve his first game into the wind. Under the circumstances, both players are therefore playing the best position in the best rotation to win the match.

When you serve with the wind, move in quickly. The ball will be coming back more slowly than usual, and a ball normally volleyed near the service line would now bounce at your feet. Getting to the net quickly allows you to take the ball in the air with the wind providing the power.

Be careful of your toss, because the ball will be pulling away from you, causing you to hit into the net. If you find yourself going after the ball, then foot faults become a problem. Alter your toss to compensate for the speed of the wind to achieve your most normal serving motion.

When you toss *into* the wind, be sure to test your toss just as you would if serving with the wind. If you toss the ball as usual, the wind will push it behind you. This will not only diminish the power of your serve but will also completely destroy the rhythm and body movement that gets you smoothly to the net. Toss the ball well out in front to alleviate this problem. The object is to hit the ball at the same time and place as you do in your regular serve. When you can control your toss, the only advantage you lose is power.

You must be very quick getting to the net, because the ball will be coming back with the wind. If you get trapped in no-man's-land, behind the service line, you lose your serving advantage in having to hit off the ground or volley up from far back. Either way, you are on the defense and the wind has caused the coup.

When you find yourself in a wind that is blowing steadily crosscourt, drive the ball hard into the wind from one side and hit for the center of the court from the other, using the wind to carry the ball to the sidelines. There is deception in this, which causes indecision on the part of your opponents. Soft, spinning shots will float around and bounce all over the court, breaking your opponents' rhythm by catching them out of position. The wind can be your friend; use it.

Then there will be those times when the wind will not be coming from any particular direction but will be exploding all over the court at the worst possible moments. There will be no pattern to it, so you cannot plan your play either with it or against it.

This is the time to keep a cool head and play your own game. The wind will be just as much a monster for your opponents as it is for you, and the players with the greatest poise will prevail.

chapter ten

drills

The following drills should be practiced to develop the quickness, stamina, and reflexes necessary to excel in the game of
doubles.

TWO ON ONE

Set up a triangle with one player at the center of the baseline
and the two opponents in the classic doubles position at the net.
The object is for the lone player to try to get the ball by the
netmen while they keep the ball in play with volleys and

overheads. Each time the ball goes out of play, begin again. Continue until the lone man runs out of gas. When he is no longer moving well or hitting effectively, he should change places with one of the netmen and resume play. Keep rotating until all three have had a workout.

This drill helps develop the reflexes, quickness, and speed of the lone man while the netmen practice control at the net.

HALF-COURT CROSSCOURT

With your partner or someone willing to practice with you, practice using only crosscourt play. If you are going to receive, assume the position in the court you will regularly play. Follow your returns to the net and play out the points with crosscourt play only. The player who hits anywhere except crosscourt loses the point. Play twenty points and then switch.

This drill teaches the receiver where to hit the ball, to anticipate the return, and to volley the server's volley. The server practices his serve and volley.

VOLLEY AND OVERHEAD

One player begins at the net and the other crosscourt on the baseline. Only crosscourt shots are allowed. The baseline player drives the ball at the netman, who should volley crosscourt directly back to the baseline. The baseline player then lobs crosscourt over the head of the netman, who must backpedal, hit the overhead crosscourt, and regain his position at the net for the return drive hit off his overhead. He then volleys crosscourt, and the receiver lobs. Continue this sequence until the ball is hit out of play or until the netman drops from fatigue. Switch positions and do it all over again.

This drill teaches ground strokes, lobs, volleys and smashes, while developing speed in moving forward for the volley and balance and body control when going for the overhead.

PLAYING HALF-COURT

Using only half of the court, with one man at the net and the other on the baseline play out points with the baseline player hitting any type of shot he can while the netman runs, smashes, and volleys the return. The point is lost when the ball goes out of half of the court or into the net. Play five points; then switch positions and play five more points. Move to the left half of the court and repeat the sequence.

This drill allows the baseline player to practice his ground strokes, while the netman concentrates on control of the volley and hitting overheads.

RECEIVING SECOND SERVE

Have your partner, or someone who would like to practice this routine, serve second serves to you on the side you usually play. Without previously altering your normal receiving position for a second serve, run around the ball and hit it with your forehand. Practice hitting both crosscourt and down the line. Switch positions after fifty serves so that both players will have the opportunity to serve and receive.

This drill is designed to familiarize the receiver with the moves required in running around the ball to hit a forehand return of serve.

FOUR VOLLEY

Four players take standard net positions and begin a rally. Start out slowly, hitting the ball well out in front; then speed up the play until someone misses. For variety, move closer to the net or begin farther back and work your way in.

This drill quickens reflexes, develops skill in volleying, sharpens anticipation, and teaches players to keep their eye on the ball.

103

chapter eleven

exercises

RUNNING THE LINES

Starting at the net on the center service line, run backward to the T, sidestep right to the sideline, run backward to the baseline, sidestep left across the court to the opposite sideline, run to the net and touch it, backpedal to the service line, sidestep to the T, and finally run to the net where you began. Use any variation of direction you wish, but always face the net and go all out in every direction.

One interesting variation is to play follow the leader: Two players begin at the net, facing each other. The leader starts backward, and the other player must do exactly as the leader does. The object is to follow the leader and arrive back at the net at the same time.

This exercise not only gets you into shape but also develops quickness in the footwork used in doubles.

SPRINTING

Lay out markers ten yards apart for forty yards. Sprint the forty yards as fast as you can. Jog backward to your starting mark. Sprint thirty yards and jog backward to start. Sprint twenty yards and then ten, jogging backward to the starting line each time. Run the above series without resting. When you have finished the series, rest for a few minutes and then sprint forty yards and walk back to the start. Repeat the forty-yard sprint until you have run two hundred yards. Rest. Sprint ten yards and stop, ten yards and stop, ten yards and stop until you have sprinted two hundred yards. Call it a day.

KANGAROO JUMPS

Beginning in a standard position, crouch and leap as high as possible, coming down in the same spot. Continue crouching springing up again and again.

This exercise develops the muscles used in going up after overheads.

STRETCHING EXERCISES

a. Placing your feet side by side, turn your right foot out, perpendicular to the left foot, and step one full step away. Bend your right knee as you shift your weight onto it, stretching as far as you can. Keep stretching gently, continuing for about fifteen seconds. Return to a standing position and repeat the exercise on the left side. Repeat the entire exercise four times.

b. Lie on your back with your body straight. Lift your legs straight up over your head and, keeping your legs together, touch your toes to the floor. Hold the position for a count of ten, and then bring your legs slowly back to the original position. Repeat ten times.

chapter twelve

tips on tactics

1. Stay at the net unless you are forced to the baseline.
2. Lob:
    a. when defending the baseline
    b. to break your opponents' rhythm
    c. to regain offensive court position
    d. in the third set when the game is tight
3. Move as a unit with your partner at all times.
4. Hit medium-paced approach shots after an opponent's weak volley to force an ineffective return.
5. Go for the winner when your opponents give you the middle or when they crowd the middle, leaving an open alley.

6. Hit directly at your opponent when you have an easy shot from midcourt.
7. The better server should always serve first unless the weather is a factor. Winning the first game is all-important.
8. Never give a match away. Even if you are losing 6-0, 5-0, 40-love, hang in there and give it your best. You never know when you may win.
9. Never change a winning game.
10. Always change a losing game.
11. Discover your opponents' weaknesses and play them to death.
12. Ignore all needling.
13. Always warm up before a match.
14. If the play is fast and you are behind, slow down the play. Do not be rushed.
15. Attack your opponent's strength at irregular intervals to keep him off balance and slightly unnerved.

index